Cool Hotels
Beach Resorts

teNeues

Imprint

Produced by fusion publishing GmbH, Stuttgart . Los Angeles   www.fusion-publishing.com

Editorial team: Martin Nicholas Kunz (Editor + Layout)
Sabine Beyer (Introduction), Patrice Farameh ("What's special" texts)
Viviana Guastalla (Editorial coordination)
Sabine Scholz (Text coordination), Alphagriese (Translation coordination French, English): Stéphanie Laloix (French),
Christine Grimm (US-English); Federica Benetti, Romina Russo (Italian), Yvette Gerstner, Sergio Ramos Ramos (Spanish)
Everbest Printing Co.Ltd - www.everbest.com, Jan Hausberg (Prepress + imaging)

Cover photo (location): courtesy Yasawa Island Resort (Yasawa Island Resort)
Back cover photos from top to bottom (location): William Abranowicz (Perivolas Traditional Houses), courtesy SALA
Samui Resort & Spa (SALA Samui Resort & Spa), Gavin Jackson (Kurumba), Roland Bauer (Kempinski Grand Hotel Heili-
gendamm), Martin Nicholas Kunz (Azulik)

Photos (location): Adrian Houston (La Coluccia, p.39), courtesy Amankila (Amankila), courtesy Amanyara (Amanyara),
courtesy Casa Colonial Beach & Spa (courtesy Casa Colonial Beach & Spa), courtesy Casadelmar (Casadelmar, p.29),
courtesy Farol Design Hotel (Farol Design Hotel), courtesy Frégate Island Private (Frégate Island Private), courtesy Danai
Beach Resort & Villas (Danai Beach Resort & Villas), courtesy EV (EV), courtesy GMH Hotels, Bali (The Club at The Legian),
courtesy Hotelito Desconocido (Hotelito Desconocido), courtesy Kempinski Grand Hotel Heiligendamm (Kempinski
Grand Hotel Heiligendamm, p.24), courtesy Labriz Silhouette (Labriz Silhouette), courtesy Le Meridien Lav (Le Meridien
Lav), courtesy Le Sereno Hotel (Le Sereno Hotel) courtesy MAIA Luxury Resort & Spa (MAIA Luxury Resort & Spa), courtesy
Oberoi Sahl Hasheesh (Oberoi Sahl Hasheesh), courtesy of Orient-Express Hotels Trains and Cruises (La Samanna, p.206,
207), courtesy Ponta dos Ganchos Resort (Ponta dos Ganchos Resort), courtesy Pousada Picinguaba (Pousada Picingua-
ba), courtesy SALA Samui Resort & Spa (SALA Samui Resort & Spa), courtesy The Alfajiri Villas (The Alfajiri Villas), courtesy
The Chedi Muscat (The Chedi Muscat), courtesy The Library (The Library), courtesy The Lodge at Kauri Cliff (The Lodge at
Kauri Cliff), courtesy The Oberoi Lombok (The Oberoi Lombok), courtesy Turtle Inn (Turtle Inn), courtesy Yasawa Island
Resort (Yasawa Island Resort), courtesy YTL Hotels & Properties (Pangkor Laut Resort), Danee Hazamaa (Bora Bora Nui
Resort & Spa), David Rogers (Benguerra Lodge), Gavin Jackson (Anantara Maldives, Kurumba, Saman Villas), Jean-Philippe
Piter (La Samanna, p.208, 209), Jörg Tietje (Esplendido), Markus Bachmann (Mykonos Theoxenia), Max Zambelli (Fal-
conara Charming House & Resort), Roland Bauer (Aparthotel Bommelje), Tonino Mosconi (La Coluccia, p.38, 40), Timos
Tsoukalas (Perivolas Traditional Houses, p.51, 52), William Abranowicz (Perivolas Traditional Houses, p.50, 54, 55)
All other photos by Martin Nicholas Kunz and Roland Bauer

Price orientation: € = < 200 €, €€ = 201 € – 350 €, €€€ = 351 € – 550 €, €€€€ = > 551 €

Published by teNeues Publishing Group

teNeues Verlag GmbH + Co. KG
Am Selder 37
47906 Kempen, Germany
Tel.: 0049-(0)2152-916-0
Fax: 0049-(0)2152-916-111
E-mail: books@teneues.de

teNeues Publishing Company
16 West 22nd Street
New York, NY 10010, USA
Tel.: 001-212-627-9090
Fax: 001-212-627-9511

teNeues Publishing UK Ltd.
P.O. Box 402
West Byfleet
KT14 7ZF, Great Britain
Tel.: 0044-1932-403509
Fax: 0044-1932-403514

teNeues France S.A.R.L.
93, rue Bannier
45000 Orléans, France
Tel.: 0033-2-38541071
Fax: 0033-2-38625340

Press department: arehn@teneues.de
Tel.: 0049-(0)2152-916-202

www.teneues.com

ISBN: 978-3-8327-9274-9

Bibliographic information published by Die Deutsche Bibliothek.
Die Deutsche Bibliothek lists this publication in the Deutsche Nationalbibliografie;
detailed bibliographic data is available in the Internet at http://dnb.ddb.de.

Contents   Page

Introduction

Getting there and taking off your shoes are often the same thing. The first time your naked feet touch the sand is the moment that you can forget and forgive everything: the gray weather back home, the uncomfortable ten-hour flight, and the realization that the swimming trunks you bought just for this trip didn't make it into the suitcase. As soon as the salty air gets into your nose and the murmuring of the waves goes to your head, your brain switches into a mode of euphoric relaxation. The vacation has started! The colors, the light, the air, and the search for shells captivates all of your senses. Every sea is a total work of sensory art, and every coast is an infinite world.

To ensure the greatest possible access to the turquoise-colored wonder world of water, *Anantara Maldives* has put its overwater villas on pilings in the lagoon. This means that you not only have the big blue right in front of your eyes, but can also spontaneously dive in and discover the fascinating private reef with all of its inhabitants directly in front of the door.

Seeing the ocean allows you to experience infinity—and think about your own role in it. There is rarely a better opportunity for this than on *Frégate Island Private*. You are far more likely to encounter giant turtles and dolphins on the 297-acre Seychelles Island with its 16 villas and seven powdered-sugar beaches than to meet the neighbors. In *Hotelito Desconocido*, the guests return to their havens by means of rowboats. In the stylish eco-resort on Mexico's Pacific Coast, a boat of your own is part of the basic equipment for each of the popular bungalows that can only be reached by waterway. Abstention from the telephone and WLAN guarantees splendid isolation. Pennants raised on the flagpole serve as the means of communication. The *Danai Beach Resort & Villas* champions the idea of realizing any type of guest wish, no matter what it is or how it is communicated. In the ocean-enamored exceptional hotel, a private dinner on a sandbank is even considered a routine request if it includes a pianist on the grand piano.

No matter if you dream of Lombok, Moorea, Heiligendamm, or the Costa Esmeralda, you will discover that the search for the perfect beach will give you fulfilling hours of reading—and vacations. What do you have to do for it? Just accept the gift!

Sabine Beyer

Einleitung

Ankommen und Schuhe ausziehen sind oft eins. Die erste Berührung der nackten Füße mit dem Sand ist der Moment, der alles vergessen und verzeihen lässt: das graue Wetter in der Heimat, den unbequemen Zehn-Stunden-Flug, die Erkenntnis, dass die extra gekaufte Badehose noch immer zu Hause liegt. Sobald die salzige Luft in die Nase und das Murmeln der Wellen zu Kopf steigt, schaltet das Gehirn in einen euphorischen Entspannungsmodus um. Der Urlaub hat begonnen! Farben, Licht, Luft und Muschelfunde nehmen sämtliche Sinne gefangen. Jedes Meer ist ein sensorisches Gesamtkunstwerk, jede Küste eine unendliche Welt.

Um einen größtmöglichen Zugang zur türkisfarbenen Wasserwunderwelt zu gewähren, setzte *Anantara Maldives* seine Overwater Villas auf Stelzen in die Lagune. So hat man das große Blau nicht nur direkt vor Augen, sondern kann auch spontan hineintauchen, und das faszinierende Hausriff samt Bewohnern direkt vor der Tür entdecken.

Angesichts des Ozeans erfährt man Unendlichkeit – und kann über die eigene Rolle darin nachdenken. Das gelingt selten besser als auf *Frégate Island Private*. Auf der 120 Hektar großen Seychellen-Insel mit ihren 16 Villen und sieben Puderzuckerstränden sind die Chancen, Riesenschildkröten und Delfine zu treffen, weitaus größer als die, den Nachbarn zu begegnen. Im *Hotelito Desconocido* ziehen sich Gäste rudernd zurück. In dem stylishen Ökoresort an Mexikos Pazifikküste gehört ein eigenes Boot zur Grundausstattung jener begehrten Bungalows, die nur auf dem Wasserweg erreichbar sind. Der Verzicht auf Telefon und WLAN garantiert die „Splendid Isolation". Als Kommunikationsmittel dienen am Flaggenmast gehisste Wimpel. Das *Danai Beach Resort & Villas* hat sich auf seine Fahne geschrieben, jedweden Gastwunsch zu realisieren, egal wie er lautet oder kommuniziert wird. In dem meerverliebten Ausnahmehotel gilt ein Private Diner auf einer Sandbank selbst dann als Routineanfrage, wenn ein Pianist am Flügel dazu verlangt wird.

Egal, ob Sie von Lombok, Moorea, Heiligendamm oder der Costa Esmeralda träumen, Sie werden feststellen, dass die Suche nach dem perfekten Strand Ihnen erfüllte Lesestunden – und Urlaube – schenken wird. Was Sie dazu tun müssen? Das Geschenk einfach annehmen!

Sabine Beyer

Introduction

Arriver là-bas signifie souvent enlever ses chaussures. La première fois que vos pieds nus touchent le sable est le moment où vous pouvez tout oublier, tout pardonner : le temps gris qui vous attend au retour, les dix heures de vol inconfortable, et le fait de réaliser que le maillot de bain spécialement acheté pour l'occasion n'est pas dans votre valise. Dès que l'air salé atteint vos narines et que le murmure des vagues caresse vos oreilles, votre cerveau se met en mode relaxation euphorique. Les vacances commencent ! Les couleurs, la lumière, l'air et la recherche de coquillages captivent tous vos sens. Chaque mer est une œuvre d'art totale, et chaque côte un monde infini.

Pour vous assurer le plus bel accès possible au monde bleu turquoise de l'eau, l'*Anantara Maldives* a mis ses villas sur des pilotis au-dessus du lagon. Cela signifie que non seulement vous avez la grande bleue en face de vos yeux, mais que vous pouvez spontanément décider de plonger et découvrir le récif privé fascinant avec tous ses habitants, directement devant votre porte.

Voir l'océan vous permet de vous faire une idée de l'infini, et de penser à votre propre rôle dans cette immensité. Il n'y a pas beaucoup d'endroits qui y soient plus propices que *Frégate Island Private*. Sur cette île de 120 hectares dans les Seychelles, avec ses 16 villas et ses sept plages de sable blanc, vous avez bien plus de chances de rencontrer des tortues géantes et des dauphins que vos voisins. A l'*Hotelito Desconocido*, les clients regagnent leurs petits paradis en barque. Dans cet élégant complexe hôtelier écologique sur la côte pacifique mexicaine, un bateau personnel fait partie de l'équipement de base de chacun des bungalows, qui peuvent seulement être rejoints par voie d'eau. L'absence de téléphone et d'accès internet vous garantit un merveilleux isolement, et ce sont des fanions hissés sur le mât qui servent de moyen de communication. Le *Danai Beach Resort & Villas* se fait fort de réaliser tous les souhaits des clients, quelle que soit leur nature ou la manière dont ils sont exprimés. Dans cet hôtel amoureux de la mer, un dîner privé sur la grève avec un musicien jouant sur le grand piano est même considéré comme faisant partie de la routine.

Que vous rêviez de Lombok, de Moorea, d'Heiligendamm ou de la Costa Esmeralda, vous découvrirez que la recherche de la plage parfaite vous offrira des heures de lecture (et de vacances !) captivantes. Que devez-vous faire pour cela ? Vous contenter d'accepter le cadeau !

Sabine Beyer

Introducción

Llegar y deshacerse de los zapatos es a menudo una sola cosa. El primer contacto de los pies desnudos con la arena representa el momento que nos hace olvidar y perdonarlo todo: el mal tiempo en el país de origen, el incómodo vuelo de diez horas o darse cuenta de que el bañador comprado exclusivamente para este viaje se quedó en casa. En cuanto el aire salado corre por nuestros pulmones y el murmurar de las olas circula por nuestros pensamientos, el cerebro pone en marcha un modo de relajación eufórica. ¡Las vacaciones han empezado! Los colores, la luz, el aire y las conchas encontradas copan nuestros sentidos. Cada mar es una obra de arte sensorial, cada costa es un mundo infinito.

Para garantizar el máximo acceso al misterioso mundo acuático color turquesa, *Anantara Maldives* construyó sus apartamentos de lujo apoyados en zancas sobre el agua de la laguna. De esta manera, uno no sólo ve el mar azul, sino que puede sumergirse espontáneamente en él y descubrir el fascinante arrecife y su fauna directamente a las puertas de casa.

Ante el océano uno reconoce la infinidad –y puede reflexionar sobre su propio papel en ésta. En pocos lugares puede lograrse esto mejor que en *Frégate Island Private*. En esta isla de las Seychelles de 120 hectáreas, con 16 villas y siete playas de arena fina, es mucho más probable encontrarse con tortugas gigantes y delfines que con otros vecinos humanos. En el *Hotelito Desconocido* los huéspedes encuentran la tranquilidad remando. En el refugio ecológico con estilo de la costa del pacífico en México, un barco privado forma parte del equipamiento básico de los solicitados bungaloes, que son únicamente accesibles por vía acuática. La renuncia al teléfono y a internet garantiza el espléndido aislamiento. Como medio de comunicación bastan unos banderines colgando de un mástil. El *Danai Beach Resort & Villas* se caracteriza por convertir en realidad cada deseo del huésped, sin importar cuál sea o cómo se pronuncie. En el excepcional hotel marítimo, una cena privada en un banco de arena se considera un deseo rutinario; incluso si ello requiere un pianista que toque el piano de cola.

No importa si sueña con Lombok, Moorea, Heiligendamm o la Costa Esmeralda, se dará cuenta de que la búsqueda de la playa perfecta le regalará horas de lectura –y vacaciones– plenas. ¿Qué le falta para empezar a vivirlo? ¡Aceptar el regalo, nada más!

Sabine Beyer

Introduzione

Arrivare su una spiaggia e togliersi le scarpe sono spesso un'unica cosa. Il primo contatto dei piedi nudi con la sabbia segna il momento in cui si dimentica e si perdona tutto: il brutto tempo a casa, le dieci stancanti ore di volo, l'essersi resi conto che il costume comprato apposta per la vacanza è rimasto a casa. Non appena l'aria piena di salsedine nel naso e il rumore delle onde penetra nelle orecchie, il cervello si sintonizza su un modo di vivere euforico e al contempo rilassato. La vacanza è iniziata! I colori, la luce, l'aria e le conchiglie raccolte sulla spiaggia catturano tutti i sensi. Ogni mare è un'opera d'arte da vedere, sentire, toccare, annusare e assaporare, ogni costa un mondo infinito.

Per offrire un accesso il più diretto possibile al fantastico mondo delle acque turchesi, *Anantara Maldives* accoglie i propri ospiti in ville costruite su palafitte nella laguna. Così non soltanto si ha il mare blu proprio davanti agli occhi, ma se si vuole ci si può anche immergere, e andare alla scoperta dell'affascinante scogliera e dei suoi abitanti a due passi dal proprio alloggio.

Di fronte all'oceano si entra a contatto con l'infinito – e si può riflettere sul proprio ruolo nell'universo. A questo scopo pochi altri luoghi si prestano meglio di *Frégate Island Private*, un'isola delle Seychelles di 120 ettari con 16 ville e sette spiagge di zucchero a velo dove è decisamente più facile incontrare tartarughe giganti e delfini che il proprio vicino. Nell'*Hotelito Desconocido* gli ospiti si possono ritirare nella propria privacy a colpo di remi – questo elegante eco-resort della costa pacifica del Messico, infatti, mette a disposizione una barca privata per ciascuno dei suoi ambiti bungalow raggiungibili solamente via mare. L'assenza di telefono e collegamento wifi garantiscono un meraviglioso isolamento, mentre per comunicare si utilizzano banderuole da issare sulle aste. Il *Danai Beach Resort & Villas* si pone come obiettivo quello di soddisfare tutti i desideri dei propri ospiti, qualsiasi essi siano e in qualunque modo vengano espressi. In questo esclusivo albergo sposato con il mare, una cena privata sulla spiaggia è una richiesta di routine solo se come accompagnamento viene richiesta musica suonata con un pianoforte a coda.

Che sogniate Lombok, Moorea, Heiligendamm o la Costa Esmeralda, vi renderete conto che la ricerca della spiaggia perfetta vi regalerà ore di lettura – e vacanze – meravigliose. Che cosa dovete fare voi? Nient'altro che accettare il regalo!

Sabine Beyer

9

Esplendido

Es Traves 5
07108 Puerto de Sóller
Mallorca
Spain
Phone: +34 971 631 850
Fax: +34 971 633 019
www.esplendidohotel.com

Price category: €
Rooms: 82 rooms
Facilities: Private beach, 2 swimming pools, garden, spa, bistro, conference, meeting facilities
Services: Room service, laundry service, babysitting, free wifi
Located: By the sea
Public transportation: Tram to Sóller, bus to Palma
Map: No. 1
Style: Modern vintage
What's special: Seafront hotel from the 1950's with 2 sea view swimming pools including 1 healing thermal pool, living room for listening to hotel's own massive vinyl music collection, state-of-the-art spacious lounge and library, fully equipped guestrooms.

Farol Design Hotel

Av. Rei Humberto II de Itália 7
2750–461 Cascais
Portugal
Phone: +35 12 14 82 34 90
Fax: +35 12 14 84 14 47
www.farol.com.pt

Price category: €€
Rooms: 34 rooms individually designed
Facilities: Mediterranean fusion restaurant The Mix, bar, outdoor saltwater pool, pool bar
Services: Room service, yoga & massage in summer months, laundry/dry cleaning service
Located: 5 min from central rail station Cascais, 23 km from Lisbon International Airport, 20 min from Lisbon
Public transportation: Train to Lisbon every 15 min
Map: No. 2
Style: Minimalist, modern
What's special: Completely renovated 19th century mansion with the latest modern developments, fashion designers have dressed each room, all guest suites have hydro-massage bathtubs, floor-to-ceiling windows offer splendid views over the Bay of Cascais.

Aparthotel Bommelje

Herenstraat 24
4357 AL Domburg
Zeeland
The Netherlands
Phone: +31 1 18 58 16 84
Fax: +31 1 18 58 22 18
www.bommelje.nl

Price category: €
Rooms: 68 rooms and family suites including 2 garden-suites
Facilities: Restaurant B
Services: Restaurant, bicycle-rental, strand-cabine rental
Located: In the centre of Domburg and near to the sea
Public transportation: Bus
Map: No. 3
Style: Modern interior in a classical building
What's special: Family-friendly hotel with all of the comforts of home such as kitchens, spacious bathrooms and balconies, offers special apartment suites with living rooms, cabins at the beach, Zeeland-style restaurant, high tea service.

Kempinski Grand Hotel Heiligendamm

Prof.-Dr.-Vogel-Straße 16–18
18209 Bad Doberan
Heiligendamm
Germany
Phone: +49 38 20 37 40 0
Fax: +49 38 20 37 40 74 74
www.kempinski-heiligendamm.com

Price category: €€
Rooms: 215 rooms and suites
Facilities: 4 restaurants, 3 bars, sauna world, spa, pool, ballroom
Services: Airport shuttle, babysitting services, bridal suite, packed lunches, free WLAN
Located: Directly at the beach of the Baltic Sea in Mecklenburg-Western Pomerania, near Rostock
Public transportation: Airport Rostock, train Bad Doberan
Map: No. 4
Style: Modern classic
What's special: This majestic building has a 3,000 m² wellness area in its own palatial space, including a medical spa; a separate children's area includes the Polar Bear Club with private villa and activities such as pony riding, pirate parties, and story telling.

Casadelmar

Route de Palombaggia
20137 Porto Vecchio
Corsica
France
Phone: +33 4 95 72 34 34
Fax: +33 4 95 72 34 35
www.casadelmar.fr

Price category: €€€€
Rooms: 34 rooms and suites
Facilities: Gastronomic restaurant with 1 Michelin star, pool restaurant, lounge bar
Services: Spa Carita and Decleor, hair stylist, private beach, heated outdoor swimming pool, business center
Located: 6 km from Porto Vecchio center
Public transportation: 20 km to the Airport International de Figari
Map: No. 5
Style: Design Hotel
What's special: Opulent guestrooms have stone floors and cedar-wood terrace with stunning views overlooking Porto-Vecchio Bay; wellness areas have four massage cabins, a hammam, gym and relaxation rooms; private beach, yacht mooring, heated outdoor infinity pool.

La Coluccia

Località Conca Verde
07028 Santa Teresa Gallura (SS)
Sardinia
Italy
Phone: +39 07 89 75 80 04
www.lacoluccia.it

Price category: €€
Rooms: 45 rooms
Facilities: Restaurant, bar
Services: Babysitting
Located: Directly on a private beach
Map: No. 6
Style: Contemporary design
What's special: Surrounded by a natural park, full-service spa and beauty center, swimming pool and beach service with complimentary sun-beds, umbrellas and beach towels, modern furnishings in all 45 guestrooms; seaside suites have spectacular views.

Falconara Charming House & Resort

Strada statale 215 km. 243
93011 Butera
Sicily
Italy
Phone: +39 09 34 34 90 12
www.mobygest.it

Price category: €€
Rooms: 70 rooms
Facilities: Restaurant, bar, spa, private beach
Services: Babysitting
Located: Directly on the beach
Map: No. 7
Style: Contemporary design
What's special: Private beach, includes a main modern building and a Norman castle with Old World charm; all guestrooms come with marble floors and four-poster beds; tennis court, pool, beachfront clubhouse with complete spa.

Le Meridien Lav

Grljevacka 2a
21312 Podstrana
Croatia
Phone: +385 21 500 500
Fax: +385 21 500 705
www.lemeridien.com/split

Price category: €€
Rooms: 381 rooms including suites
Facilities: 8 restaurants and bars, conference and banqueting facilities, night club, casino tennis academy, water sports center, Penguin Club for young guests, Diocletian Spa and wellness center, yacht marina
Services: 24 h room service
Located: 8 km south of Split on a 800 m beach
Public transportation: Bus to city center
Map: No. 8
Style: Understated luxury
What's special: Award-winning landscaped gardens with 800 m of shoreline, guest rooms with stunning views overlooking surrounding islands and cityscape, 8 restaurants and bars, casino, nightclub with live entertainment, Water Sports Center, Penguin Club for kids.

Danai Beach Resort & Villas

63088 Nikiti
Sithonia, Halkidiki
Greece
Phone: +30 23750 20400
Fax: +30 23750 22591
www.dbr.gr

Price category: €€€€
Rooms: 3 rooms, 52 suites, 5 villas
Facilities: Private sandy beach, seaside bar, 3 restaurants, spa, shops, gym, tennis court, water sports
Services: Babysitting, butler services, car rental
Located: Between two villages and 90 km away from the International Airport of Thessaloniki (SKG)
Public transportation: Not available, car or helicopter transfer arranged by the hotel
Map: No. 9
Style: Modern classic, elegant
What's special: Spacious suites and villas, 3 restaurants from light meals to Greek Mediterranean top gourmet in Greece, expansive selection of day and night recreation activities, luxury Moroccan-style Wellness & Spa, boat and helicopter excursions.

Mykonos Theoxenia

Kato Milli
84600 Mykonos
Greece
Phone: +30 22 89 02 22 30
Fax: +30 22 89 02 30 08
www.mykonostheoxenia.com

Price category: €€
Rooms: 52 rooms
Facilities: Restaurant, breeze in bar, breeze out bar, healthy club, Saint Charalambos chapel
Services: Secretary, doctor's attention, daily press, transport to and from the airport, organization of wedding receptions, christenings, birthdays, anniversaries
Located: On the cosmopolitan island of Mykonos
Public transportation: Bus
Map: No. 10
Style: Sixties inspired
What's special: Boutique hotel with retro 1960's style, located close to the glamorous Mykonos nightlife, 40-seat creative area called "the board", "bhealthy club" spa, gourmet Mediterranean cuisine on the waterfront terrace restaurant.

Perivolas Traditional Houses

84702 Oia
Santorini
Greece
Phone: +30 228 607 1308
Fax: +30 228 607 1309
www.perivolas.gr

Price category: €€€
Rooms: 20 suites
Facilities: Swimming pool, restaurant, bar
Services: Concierge, transfers, room service, parking
Located: On the cliff overlooking the Caldera
Public transportation: Bus
Map: No. 11
Style: Relaxing haven with breathtaking views
What's special: Preserving the integrity of the original old cave houses this luxurious and exclusive retreat stands out for its immaculate minimalist aesthetic and peaceful and informal ambience, the perfect romantic hideaway in Santorini.

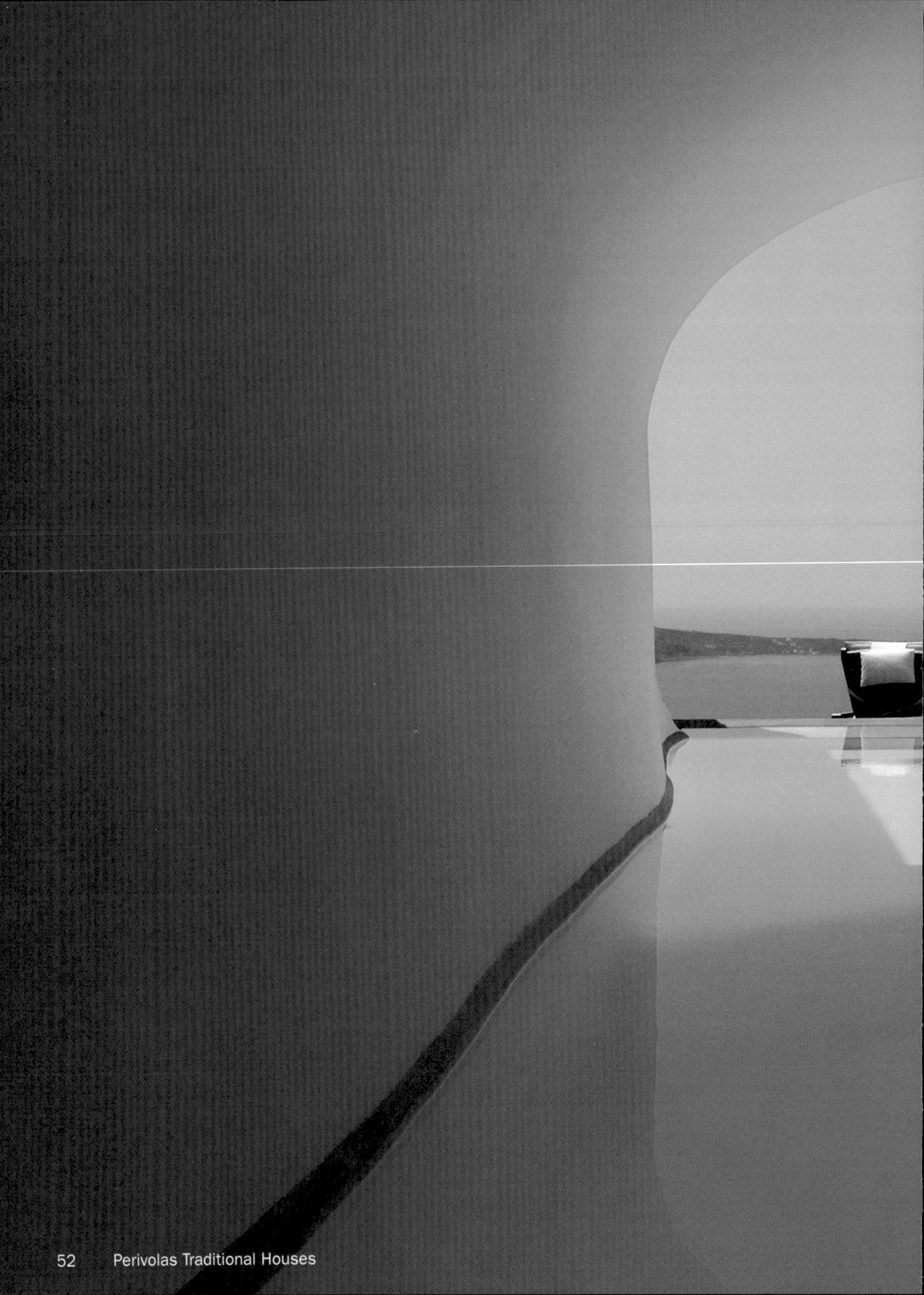

Fax: +90 25 23 77 55 66
www.evhotels.com.tr

Located: On the hill of a very reserved area overlooking Türkbükü bay, 40 km from Bodrum International Airport
Map: No. 12
Style: Hip boutique hotel
What's special: Exclusive hilltop private hideaway overlooking stunning views of the Türkbükü bay, full service wellness community, exclusive deck beach, 48 ultra-stylish spacious residential homes designed in modern white, each villa shares one of the 9 swimming pools but with its own living room, terrace, and kitchen.

Oberoi Sahl Hasheesh

117, Hurghad
Red Sea
Egypt
Phone: +20 65 3440 777
Fax: +20 65 3440 788
www.oberoisahlhasheesh.com

Price category: €€
Rooms: 63 Deluxe Suites, 21 Superior Deluxe Suites, 12 Grand Suites, 6 Royal Suites
Facilities: The Restaurant, The Pergola, Zaafran Restaurant, The Bar, spa & fitness
Services: 24 h room service, Mercedes E 200 cars for rent
Located: A secluded heaven on the Red Sea Coast
Public transportation: Mercedes guest service on request
Map: No. 13
Style: Resplendent with domes, arches and columns
What's special: All-suite Arabian-style luxury resort on the Red Sea Coast set on private beach that spans over 19 hectars, complete privacy with 102 separate spacious villas with own courtyards; some bathrooms look out into a small garden with outside shower; pampering treatments from Oberoi Spa.

The Alfajiri Villas

Ukunda
Diani Beach
Kenya
Phone: +254 733 630 491
Fax: +254 403 203 466
www.alfajirivillas.com

Price category: €€€€
Rooms: 2 villas for 8 persons and 1 villa for 4 persons
Facilities: Infinity pool, private veranda
Services: Massage, yoga, golf; English speaking nannies, private butler and chef, driver at disposal
Located: On the south coast in Diani, 1 h from Mombasa Airport
Map: No. 14
Style: Fascinating mix of luxury and rustic; furniture designed and made by Marika Molinaro
What's special: Three luxurious villas overlooking the Indian Ocean amidst breezy palms garden, tasteful decoration blend of African and Far Eastern art craft and newly designed and handmade furniture, most romantic ocean view rooms, utter privacy and impeccable service.

Benguerra Lodge   71

The Chedi Muscat

Al Khuwair
Gubrah
133 Muscat
Sultanate of Oman
Phone: +96 8 24 52 44 00
Fax: +96 8 24 49 34 85
www.ghmhotels.com

Price category: €€€
Rooms: 156 rooms
Facilities: 3 restaurants, 2 poolside cabanas, spa, private beach, 2 swimming pools, 2 flood-lit tennis courts, The Library, boutique, fine arts gallery
Services: 24 h room service
Located: On the stunning Bouschar beachfront in Oman, where crystal water mirror images of mountain ranges
Public transportation: Taxi
Map: No. 16
Style: Blend of Omani architecture and Asian Zen style
What's special: Stylish takes on Omani architecture with Oriental minimalist design, exquisite gardens with tranquil ponds; infinity pool with gazebos offers panoramic views of the Gulf of Oman, Chedi Club Suites feature huge sunken terrazzo bathtubs and a terrace or balcony.

Frégate Island Private

Frégate Private Island
Seychelles
Indian Ocean
Phone: +49 69 860 042 980
Fax: +49 69 860 042 981
www.fregate.com

Price category: €€€€
Rooms: 16 villas with pool, max 40 guests
Facilities: Restaurant Frégate House, Plantation House Restaurant, Pirates Bar, Anse Bambous Beach Bar, 2 public pools, tree house, wine cellar, The Rock Spa, private beach limited to max 40 guests to protect the endemic wildlife (turtles, birds)
Services: Nature excursions, babysitting
Located: Private island at 20 min flight from Mahé
Public transportation: Helicopter and boat service
Map: No. 17
Style: Natural luxury
What's special: Completely exclusive island with 16 villas positioned for absolute privacy, no day visitors allowed on island; each villa has an outdoor dining pavilion and a large terrace with a day bed and a private pool.

House of Ansuya, 2nd floor
Mahé
Seychelles
Indian Ocean
Phone: +248 293 949
Fax: +248 293 939
www.labriz-seychelles.com

Price category: €
Rooms: 110 Villas, 1 Presidential Suite
Facilities: Creole restaurant, Italian restaurant, grilled seafood and Teppanyaki restaurant, café, lounge, spa, dive school, eco center, none motorized watersports
Services: Babysitting on request, 24 h reception, 24 h villa dining, CD/DVD library, medical center
Located: 45 min boat or 15 min helicopter from Mahé
Public transportation: Boat transfer from Mahé approx. 1 h
Map: No. 18
Style: Modern colonial style; luxury, contemporary design
What's special: Luxury villas set between a lush tropical forest and sandy beach, 6 restaurants; 17 pavilions have private gardens, some beach villas have private plunge pools, pavilion suites available for private spa treatments or romantic dinners.

MAIA Luxury Resort & Spa

Anse Louis, Mahé
Seychelles
Indian Ocean
Phone: +248 390 000
Fax: +248 355 476
www.maia.com.sc

Price category: €€€€
Rooms: 30 villas spacious hilltop and beachfront each with private pool and uninterrupted ocean view
Facilities: Gourmet restaurant Tec-Tec, sunset pool bar, Spa by La Prairie
Services: Dedicated butler service per villa
Located: On 12 hectar beachfront of powder-white sand
Public transportation: 25 min chauffeured drive to and from Mahé airport arranged by the hotel
Map: No. 19
Style: Asian style, state-of-the-art technology
What's special: Super-luxurious thatched-roof villas have living areas with daybeds, infinity pool and pantries, in-villa barbeque dining option; main hotel areas such as the restaurant and the open air Maia spa are reached by chauffeured buggy.

Constance Belle Mare Plage

Belle Mare
Poste de Flacq
Mauritius
Indian Ocean
Phone: +230 402 26 00
Fax: +230 402 26 26
www.bellemareplagehotel.com

Price category: €€
Rooms: 92 Prestige Rooms, 137 Junior Suites, 6 Deluxe Suites, 20 villas and 1 Presidential Villa
Facilities: 7 restaurants, 7 bars, Shiseido's Qi method spa, private beach protected by an offshore coral reef, ideal for swimming, watersports and snorkeling
Services: Kakoo Club for 4 to 12 years old children
Located: On 2 km white sandy beach
Public transportation: Taxi
Map: No. 20
Style: Modern chic
What's special: White-stucco resort set on 20 tropical gardens acres, golfer's dream with two championship 18-hole courses, two beauty and wellness centers; separate villas have their own entrance and private heated pool for utmost privacy.

Taj Exotica Mauritius

Wolmar, Flic en Flac
Mauritius
Indian Ocean
Phone: +230 403 1500
Fax: + 230 453 5555
www.tajhotels.com

Price category: €€€€
Rooms: 65 private villas
Facilities: Coast2Coast all day dining restaurant, Cilantro Panasian and Indian restaurant, bar & lounge, spa, fitness center, swimmingpool, tennis court, boutique
Services: 24 h room and butler service, laundry service, mini club with pirate ship
Located: Spread over 11 scenic hectars overlooking the serene, blue waters of Tamarin Bay
Public transportation: Limousine & helicopter transfers
Map: No. 21
Style: Beach-side getaway in Colonial Mauritian architecture
What's special: Most luxurious use of the indoor-outdoor design philosophy, living spaces covered by huge thatched-roofs, some of the 65 villas with private plunge pools, free daily meditation session.

Anantara Maldives

Dhigufinolhu
South Male Atoll
Male
The Maldives
Phone: +96 664 4100
Fax: +96 664 4101
www.maldives.anantara.com

Price category: €€€
Rooms: Anantara Dhigu 70 beach villas and 40 over-water suites, Anantara Veli 50 overwater bungalows
Facilities: 8 restaurants, 2 bars, 2 spas, diving/water sports
Services: Dining by Design in your dream location
Located: Spread over two idyllic islands
Public transportation: 35 min by private speedboat from Male International Airport
Map: No. 22
Style: Maldivian Design and Artwork
What's special: Two idyllic resorts on 2 hectars island of walled lush gardens and peaceful shores of sandy beach, Anantara Veli with coconut-thatched bungalows set above coral, Anantara Dhigu with luxurious suites and villas some of which have a large two-person terrazzo bathtub by the lagoon or a private turquoise plunge pool.

Kurumba

Vihamanafushi
North Male Atoll
The Maldives
Phone: +960 33 32 26 2
Fax: +960 33 25 30 1
www.kurumba.com

Price category: €€€
Rooms: 180 bungalows and villas
Facilities: 6 restaurants, 2 bars, Aquum spa, sports center (including yoga), table tennis, tennis court, water sports center, diving school, conference rooms
Services: 24 h reception and room service, medical center, laundry, babysitting, excursions, night fishing
Located: On a white sand beach
Public transportation: Speed boat
Map: No. 23
Style: Elegantly inspired by Maldivian architecture
What's special: Luxury island resort set in nurtured tropical gardens and on intimate white beaches. A house reef with exotic marine life makes Kurumba a snorkeling dreamworld. Aquum spa merges east with west using all natural ingredients.

Saman Villas

Aturuwella
Bentota
Sri Lanka
Phone: +94 3 42 27 54 35
Fax: +94 3 42 27 54 33
www.samanvilla.com

Price category: €€€€
Rooms: 26 suites and 1 villa
Facilities: Swimming pool, manicured cascading gardens, 2 Sri Lankan cuisine restaurants, lounge bar, bar, snooker table, table tennis, badminton
Services: Evening entertainment arranged on most evenings, including ballet and soothing instrumental music
Located: On the beach
Map: No. 24
Style: Sri Lankan
What's special: Luxurious suites with terrace or balcony and day bed with spectacular views over sea and open-air bathrooms with courtyard, stocked library, full-service spa, infinity pool and relaxing gardens, one two-story villa for maximum privacy.

The Leela Kempinski Goa

Mobor, Cavelossim, Salcette
403701 Goa
India
Phone: +91 83 22 87 12 34
Fax: +91 83 22 87 13 52
www.theleela.com

Price category: €€€
Rooms: 185 rooms and suites
Facilities: 4 restaurants, 3 bars, discotheque, swimming pool, badminton, watersports, 12-hole par-3 golf course, flood-lit tennis courts, Ayurvedic center, gaming club
Services: Children's activity center, babysitting on request, yoga and meditation classes
Located: Surrounded by the Arabian sea and River Sal
Map: No. 25
Style: Ancient Indian
What's special: Indian-style luxury resort set on 30 hectars of lush gardens with lotus pools and a small waterfall. All rooms are spacious and elegant, with private balconies for you to enjoy a relaxing breakfast or a romantic dinner looking the lagoon.

SALA Samui Resort and Spa

10/9 Moo 5, Baan Plai Laem
Bophut, Koh Samui
Suratthani 84320
Thailand
Phone: +66 77 245 888
Fax: +66 77 245 889
www.salasamui.com

Price category: €€€€
Rooms: 69 villas and suites of which 53 have private swimming pools
Facilities: 2 restaurants, 2 bars, wine cellar, 2 beachfront swimming pools
Services: Thai cooking classes, pillow and soap selection
Located: On the beach, 10 min to airport and Chaweng
Public transportation: Taxi, transfers arranged by the hotel
Map: No. 26
Style: Traditional Thai architecture and modern design
What's special: Deluxe beachfront resort with private swimming pools and open-air outdoor bathroom, personalized service, Mandara spa and fitness gym, 25 m lap pool surrounded by 4 massage salas floating in a beautiful lotus pond.

The Library

14/1 Moo2, Chaweng Beach
Koh Samui
Thailand
Phone: +62 3 61 73 06 22
Fax: +62 3 61 73 06 23
www.thelibrary.name

Price category: €€
Rooms: 13 suites and 13 studios
Facilities: Beach Bar, The Page Restaurant, fitness center, The Library
Services: Babysitting, one-on-one service, personal assistant service
Located: In the center of Chaweng beach, the most popular commercial area in Samui
Public transportation: Taxi
Map: No. 27
Style: Semi-minimalist, modern
What's special: Beachfront hotel divided into 26 modern cabins, open-air restaurant, expansive collection of books, music and movies; many suites include jacuzzis and bathtubs with rain showers, fitness area has 270 degree ocean view; unique red swimming pool.

Pangkor Laut Resort

Pangkor Laut Private Island
Perak
Malaysia
Phone: +30 22 89 02 22 30
Fax: +30 22 89 02 30 08
www.pangkorlautresort.com

Price category: €€€
Rooms: 148 garden hill and sea villas
Facilities: 3 restaurants, 3 bars, 2 swimming pools, jet pool and cold dip, gym, 3 tennis courts, squash court, spa, hair salon, spa boutique, library, gift shop, conference and banquet hall
Services: In-room-dining and babysitting
Located: On a privately owned island located 5 km off the West Coast of Malaysia along the Straits of Malacca
Public transportation: 45 min ferry from Lumut
Map: No. 28
Style: Tropical-malay
What's special: Privately-owned 121 hectar island, private over-water bungalows, five-star food served in 5 different restaurants, world renowned spa; 8 exclusive estates have private access to the beach and swimming pools.

The Club at The Legian

Jalan Laksmana, Seminyak Beach
80361 Bali
Indonesia
Phone: +62 3 61 73 06 22
Fax: +62 3 61 73 06 23
www.ghmhotels.com

Price category: €€€
Rooms: 10 one-bedroom villas, 1 three-bedroom villa, each with a 10 m private pool
Facilities: The Club Lounge, 35 m lap swimming pool, use of The Legian Hotel facilities including spa, gym, pool
Services: Children menu, cardboard games, 24 h room service, private butler and complimentary laundry service
Located: Set in tastefully designed enclave to main hotel
Public transportation: Shuttle service
Map: No. 29
Style: Exclusive design by Jaya Ibrahim
What's special: A truly private, exclusive environment amidst the serenity of Bali's natural landscape. Each building is surrounded by a wide, teak-floored veranda and flanked by water features. Each villa is appointed its own private butler – the ultimate in personalized service.

The Club at The Legian   137

Amankila

Manggis, Karangesam
80871 Bali
Indonesia
Phone: +62 36 34 13 33
Fax: +62 36 34 15 55
www.amanresorts.com

Price category: €€€
Rooms: 34 free-standing suites
Facilities: Restaurant, bar, The Beach Club, private beach, library, boutique, spa, three-tiered swimming pool
Services: Yoga classes amongst the coconut trees
Located: Set on a cliff side overlooking the Lombok Strait in East Bali
Public transportation: not available
Map: No. 30
Style: Contemporary Balinese
What's special: Exclusive tropical hideaway resort with stunning ocean views and peaceful cliff-side setting with multi-tiered infinity pools, beach club with 8 private lounging canopied beds, oversized daybeds in the library, pampering spa treatments in the suites, in the designated massage pavilion or in a secluded area of the beach club.

The Oberoi Lombok

Medana Beach, Tanjung
83001 Mataram
West Lombok
Indonesia
Phone: +62 3 70 63 84 44
Fax: +62 3 70 63 24 96
www.oberoihotels.com

Price category: €€€
Rooms: 50 rooms, including 30 pavilions and 20 villas
Facilities: Tokek Bar, Sunbird Café, Lumbung Restaurant, tennis court, freshwater pool, spa, sauna, jacuzzi, gym, beauty salon, library, boutique, travel agency
Services: Babysitting, beach club with PADI certification, laundry and dry cleaning
Located: On north west coast of Lombok, 33 km from airport, 28 km from Mataram city
Public transportation: Car transfers provided by the hotel
Map: No. 31
Style: Modern yet luxurious
What's special: A tropical hideaway set among 10 hectars of landscaped gardens with a private beach, villas with thatched-roofs, terraced pavilions with large terraces overlooking the sea, full-service health spa, fitness center.

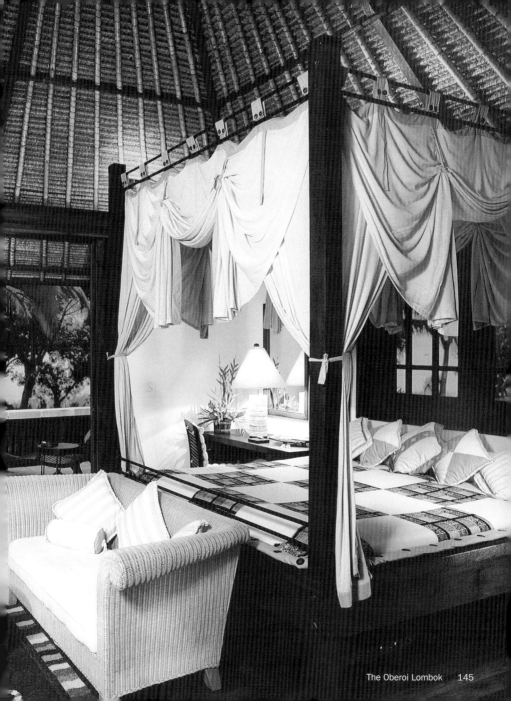

The Lodge at Kauri Cliffs

Matauri Bay Road
Matauri Bay
Northland
New Zealand
Phone: +64 9 407 0010
Fax: +64 9 407 0061
www.kauricliffs.com

Price category: €€€€
Rooms: 11 cottages comprising of 16 Deluxe Suites and 6 Suites, 2 Bedroom Owner's Cottage
Facilities: Gourmet à la carte dining restaurant, 2 tennis courts, swimming pool with spa, fitness center, 3 secluded swimming beaches
Services: Room service on request
Located: Near Matauri Bay, Northland
Public transportation: 45 min flight from Auckland
Map: No. 32
Style: Luxury colonial
What's special: Beautiful colonial residence with surrounding cottages, professional 18-hole golf course, 3 km of beach shoreline, infinity-edge swimming pool, world class spa, fitness center, 3 secluded swimming beaches.

Sheraton Moorea Lagoon Resort and Spa

Papetoai
Moorea
French Polynesia
Phone: +689 55 1111
Fax: +689 55 1155
www.sheratonmoorea.com
www.sheraton.com/moorea

Price category: €€€€
Rooms: 54 overwater, 52 garden and beach bungalows
Facilities: Restaurant, Rotui Bar & Grill, The Eimeo Bar, The Toata Bar, tournament tennis courts, fitness facility
Services: Daily live entertainment throughout the resort starting at sunset
Located: Between two bays on heart-shaped Moorea
Public transportation: 10 min flight or 30 min catamaran ride from Tahiti
Map: No. 33
Style: Romantic luxury
What's special: Polynesian-style resort on a private lagoon, beachside pool with bar and grill, spa; bungalows have luxurious interiors with claw-foot bathtubs and walk-in showers, over-the-water-bungalows have glass areas to watch tropical fish swimming below.

Bora Bora Nui Resort & Spa

Motu Toopua, Nunue
Bora Bora
French Polynesia
Phone: +689 603 300
Fax: +689 603 301
www.boraboranui.com

Price category: €€€€
Rooms: 16 Lagoon Suites, 101 Villas , 3 Royal Villas
Facilities: Infinity swimming pool, panoramic hilltop spa, fitness center with sauna and hammam
Services: Romantic Polynesian weddings and beach side dinners, 24 h room service
Located: Built around a sacred and legendary cove of white sand and majestic lava rock
Map: No. 34
Style: Combination of Polynesian tradition and sumptuous comfort
What's special: Built along a hillside this resort offers stunning 360° views, hilltop spa pampers you with traditional island beauty secrets and ingredients; unforgettable vanilla and island flowers scents.

Yasawa Island Resort

Yasawa Island
Yasawa Group of Islands
Fiji
Phone: +679 6722 266
Fax: +679 6724 456
www.yasawa.com

Price category: €€€€
Rooms: 18 rooms
Facilities: Lounge, bar, restaurant, boutique, baravi spa, swimming pool, tennis court, beach volleyball
Services: Snorkeling, light handline fishing, kayaks, catamarans, windsurfing, romantic beach picnics, bush walking, safari drives, Blue Lagoon Caves visit
Located: On the beach
Public transportation: 35 min air transfer from Nadi to Yasawa Island Resort serviced with own air-strip
Map: No. 35
Style: Exclusive and contemporary Fijian Styles
What's special: Remote island with 18 thatched-roof beach huts, beachside Baravi Spa, private picnics on deserted beaches, superb diving; all bungalows have luxury interiors with traditional art and open air showers.

Shutters on the Beach

One Pico Blvd.
Santa Monica CA, 90405
California
USA
Phone: +1 310 458 0030
Fax: +1 310 458 4589
www.shuttersonthebeach.com

Price category: €€€€
Rooms: 186 guest rooms and 12 suites
Facilities: One Pico Restaurant, Coast Beach Café and Bar, spa, pool, jacuzzi, fitness center, health club
Services: 24 h room service, fireplace in rooms, minibar, Internet access, whirlpool, DVD and newspaper
Located: Sits perfectly on the sand of Santa Monica Bay
Public transportation: Big Blue Bus, Santa Monica Bus Line 1
Map: No. 36
Style: Traditional architecture of America's historic beach resorts during the 1920s and 1930s
What's special: Beachfront hotel where each guest room is designed like a private beach cottage with balconies with ocean views, expansive spa menu at ONE, pool deck, ocean terrace with 2 fireplaces and full service.

The Setai

2001 Collins Avenue
Miami Beach FL 33139
Florida
USA
Phone: +1 305 520 6000
US Toll Free: +888 625 7500
Fax: +1 305 520 6600
www.setai.com

Price category: €€€€
Rooms: 125 rooms
Facilities: Spa, 3 pools, hot tub, fitness center, courtyard, Asian influenced boutique, a 27 m long poolside bar, restaurant, grill, the Pool Beach Bar
Services: Room service, 24 h concierge, kids services/babysitting, Internet access, pets allowed, laundry, valet
Located: Beach front
Public transportation: Bus, taxi, rental car
Map: No. 37
Style: Contemporary and Asian design
What's special: Elegant hotel is also luxury residential tower on popular South Beach, contemporary Zen feeling with ultra-modern minimalist design and Asian art; rooms have spacious granite baths and rainfall showers, pools have areas with different water temperature.

Hotelito Desconocido

Playón de Mismaloya
48360 Cruz de Loreto
Puerto Vallarta
Mexico
Phone: +52 322 281 4010
Fax: +52 322 281 4130
www.hotelito.com

Price category: €€
Rooms: Rustic open-air suites
Facilities: 2 restaurants, El Cantarito on the estuary and El Nopalito on the beach
Services: Housekeeping service, bottled pure drinking water, biodegradable bathroom amenities, concierge
Located: 97 km south from Puerto Vallarta, part of the natural reserve of Playon de Mismaloya
Public transportation: Private transfer on request
Map: No. 38
Style: Natural cozy
What's special: Ecology-conscious hotel built with indigenous designs; solar-powered bungalows stand where the lagoon meets the sea on a wetland estuary in a nature reserve with 150 birds species and three different turtles species; saltwater pool, natural spa.

Azulik

Carretera Tulum, Ruinas Km 5
Zona Hotelera
Tulum, Quintana Roo
Mexico
Phone: +54 11 59 18 64 00
Fax: +54 11 59 18 64 99
www.ecotulum.com

Price category: €€
Rooms: 15 private villas
Facilities: Restaurant, bar, spa, temazcal, dry floatation tank shared with next door eco friendly resort Copal
Services: Room service, parking, indoor massages, tours and information services, kayak and snorkel rentals
Located: 1.5 h from Cancun's airport, 6 km from Tulum's town, 8 km from the ruins
Public transportation: Only private transportation
Map: No. 39
Style: Eco Chic Retreat
What's special: Ecology-conscious luxury resort with 15 private cabanas with spectacular views of the Caribbean Sea, built among 0,8 hectar of lush tropical gardens; ocean-front villas have hand-carved wooden bathtubs, Maya Spa also offers early morning yoga.

Turtle Inn

Placencia Village
Stann Creek District
Belize
Phone: +501 824 4914
Fax: +501 824 4913
www.blancaneaux.com

Price category: €€€
Rooms: 8 villas, 17 cottages
Facilities: 3 restaurants, 2 bars, 2 pools, dive shop
Services: Spa services, tour desk, babysitting
Located: Beachfront property just north of Placencia village in southern Belize
Public transportation: Regular scheduled flights from Belize City
Map: No. 40
Style: Balinese influenced with local sustainable materials
What's special: Small luxury private hotel owned by Francis Ford Coppola; villas are few steps from the 200 m of shoreline; open-air restaurant, twelve palm-thatched villas and cabanas with artisan crafted furnishings, outdoor garden showers, personal butlers.

hectars providing some of the world's best wall and reef diving; villas have large central living area and private plunge pools, private staff, 50 m stone pool.

Casa Colonial Beach & SPA

Playa Dorada
Puerto Plata
Dominican Republic
Phone: +809 320 2111
Fax: +809 320 4017

Price category: €€
Rooms: 50 suites
Facilities: Lobby-lounge and bar, top gourmet restaurant Lucia with view to the mangrove lagoon, wedding pavilion, gym with scheduled pilate and yoga classes
Services: Room service until 11 pm, laundry service, private transfer to 18-hole Robert Trent golf course
Located: On north coast of the Dominican Republic
Public transportation: Taxi
Map: No. 42
Style: Old-world elegance with contemporary style
What's special: Seaside resort located directly on the water, old-world colonial with contemporary style with most modern amenities; Bagua spa has 13 treatment rooms; beach resort club, access to golf course, rooftop sundeck with infinity pool and 4 jacuzzis, family-friendly.

Le Sereno Hotel

Grand-cul-de-sac
97133 Saint-Barthélemy
French Antilles
Phone: +590 590 298 300
Fax: +590 590 277 547
www.lesereno.com

Price category: €€
Rooms: 37 rooms
Facilities: Restaurant des Pêcheurs, Le Sereno Bar and Lounge, beach club, swimming pool, boutique
Services: 24 h room service, in room spa treatment
Located: On the East end of the island along 180 m of beach, protected from the ocean waves by a coral reef
Public transportation: 45 min high-speed boat, 10 min flight to Saint Barthélemy, limousine to the airport
Map: No. 43
Style: Modern and elegant custom furnishing
What's special: Intimate hotel designed by Christian Liaigre with only 37 suites with stunning views of the tranquil Grand-cul-de-sac bay, 183 m of palm-shaded beach; fashionable guest rooms come with plasma televisions and in-room iPods; in-room spa treatments.

La Samanna

97064 St Martin
French West Indies
Phone: +590 590 87 64 00
Fax: +590 590 87 87 86
www.lasamanna.com

Price category: €€€€
Rooms: 81 ocean view villas, suites, rooms
Facilities: 2 restaurants, 2 bars, state-of-the-art fitness center, serene indoor/outdoor spa, the only Pilates studio in the Caribbean, 3 tennis courts, infinity pool
Services: 24 h room service
Located: On 22 hectars of pristine, beachfront property, 15 min from Marigot, St Martin's capital
Map: No. 44
Style: Creole culture inspired design
What's special: Oceanfront resort set on lush gardens overlooking 22 hectars of beach, curtained beach cabanas equipped with TV, Elysées Spa surrounded by relaxing gardens; some suites have private rooftop sundecks, treatment rooms have private outdoor shower.

Anse Chastanet

Soufriere
St Lucia's Caribbean West coast
Phone: +758 459 7000
Fax: +758 459 7700
www.ansechastanet.com

Price category: €€
Rooms: 49 rooms including 12 beachside rooms
Facilities: 2 restaurants, 2 bars, 2 beaches, spa, five star dive center, house reef, snorkeling, ocean kayaks, non motorised watersports including sunfish, mountain bikes
Services: Weddings and vow renewals, day yacht charter, airport transfers, tours including whale watching
Located: Beachfront amidst tropical foliage
Public transportation: 15 min drive or water taxi from Soufriere
Map: No. 45
Style: Unique open wall rooms
What's special: Individually designed rooms, some of which have one open wall extending into a large infinity pool with stunning views over Piton mountains, open-floor designed bathrooms with chromatherapy whirlpool tubs.

Ponta dos Ganchos Resort

Rua Eupidio Alves do
Nascimento, 104
City of Governador Celso Ramos
Brazil
Phone: +55 48 32 62 50 00
Fax: +55 48 32 62 50 46
www.pontadosganchos.com.br

Price category: €€€€
Rooms: 25 bungalows, 6 categories
Facilities: Beach, indoor heated swimming pool, tennis court, games room, snooker room, fitness center, boutique, cinema, restaurant, bars, business center
Services: 24 h reception, DVD library, laundry
Located: On a private peninsula on Brazil's south coast, 40 km north of Florianópolis Island in Santa Catarina
Public transportation: Bus and taxis available, hotel recommends private transfer, helicopter or boat
Map: No. 46
Style: Contemporary design
What's special: 25 bungalows set deep into the lush rainforest vegetation with ocean views, some with private plunge pools, saunas, and jacuzzis, spa by Christian Dior, massage tents, nature trails.

Pousada Picinguaba

Vila Picinguaba
Rua G, 130
11680-000 Ubatuba-SP
State of Sao Paulo
Brazil
Phone: +55 12 38 36 91 05
Fax: +55 12 38 36 91 03
www.picinguaba.com

Price category: €€
Rooms: 9 double rooms and 1 honeymoon suite
Facilities: Restaurant, private schooner, pool, home theater, sauna
Services: Transportation and guide services
Located: Half-way between Rio and São Paolo, in a peaceful bay at the heart of a Natural Park
Public transportation: Bus from São Paulo or Rio to Paraty, then taxi to Vila Picinguaba
Map: No. 47
Style: Rustic and charming
What's special: Ten charming suites in this first class hideaway set in a lush rainforest overlooking the bay, retreat for adventure seekers with local guides for jungle hikes; hotel's 12 m schooner take guests to nearby islands; candle-lit dinners with fresh Brazilian cuisine.

No.	Hotel	Page

Other titles by teNeues

ISBN 978-3-8327-9237-4

ISBN 978-3-8327-9247-3

ISBN 978-3-8327-9234-3

ISBN 978-3-8327-9243-5

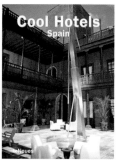

ISBN 978-3-8327-9230-5

ISBN 978-3-8327-9248-0

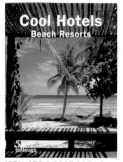

ISBN 978-3-8327-9274-9

Interior image **Cool Hotels Beach Resorts**

Styleguides: Size: **15 x 19 cm**, 6 x 7 ½ in., 224 pp., **Flexicover**, c. 200 color photographs,
Text: English / German / French / Spanish / Italian
www.teneues.com

Other titles by teNeues

ISBN 978-3-8327-9206-0   ISBN 978-3-8327-9207-7   ISBN 978-3-8327-9205-3

Cool Hotels City: Size: **15 x 19 cm**, 6 x 7½ in., 160 pp., **Flexicover**, c. 200 color photographs,
Text: English / German / French / Spanish / Italian

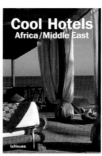

ISBN 978-3-8327-9105-6   ISBN 978-3-8327-9051-6   ISBN 978-3-8238-4565-2

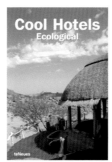

ISBN 978-3-8327-9134-6   ISBN 978-3-8327-9135-3   ISBN 978-3-8327-9203-9

Designpockets: Size: **13.5 x 19 cm**, 5¼ x 7½ in., 400 pp., **Flexicover**, c. 400 color photographs,
Text: English / German / French / Spanish / Italian

www.teneues.com

Other titles by teNeues

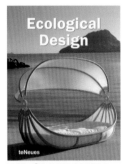

ISBN 978-3-8327-9229-9

Interior image **Ecological Design**

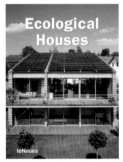

ISBN 978-3-8327-9227-5

Interior image **Ecological Houses**

ISBN 978-3-8327-9228-2

Interior image **Garden Design**

Styleguides: Size: **15 x 19 cm**, 6 x 7 ½ in., 224 pp., **Flexicover**, c. 200 color photographs,
Text: English / German / French / Spanish / Italian

www.teneues.com